The

New

Body

University of Pittsburgh Press

The New Body

James Moore

Library of Congress Cataloging in Publication Data

Moore, James, birth date
  The new body.

  (Pitt poetry series)
  Poems.
  I. Title.
PS3563.0618N4   811'.5'4   75-9125
  ISBN 0-8229-5260-2

"The New Man," "Sunset," and "Doors" first appeared in *Ironwood*. "3 A.M./
New Moon," "Loneliness," and "The Hidden Knot" were originally published
in *Chelsea 34*. Some of the other poems in this volume have appeared in *25
Minnesota Poets*, *Dacotah Territory*, *The Nation*, *The Seventies*, *Hanging Loose*,
The Greenfield Review, and *Words from the House of the Dead* (Greenfield
Review Press). All are reprinted by permission of the publishers.

The epigraph to "In the book *Oriental Mythologies*" is taken from "There Is,"
Copyright © 1961 by Louis Simpson. Reprinted from *At the End of the Open
Road*, by Louis Simpson, by permission of Wesleyan University Press. The epi-
graph to "There can be no revolution without the grave" is taken from "Medusa,"
by Louise Bogan, from *The Blue Estuaries*, published by Farrar, Straus &
Giroux, copyright © 1968.

The publication of this book is supported by a grant from the National Endowment for the Arts in Washington, D.C., a Federal Agency.

For Patricia Hampl

CONTENTS

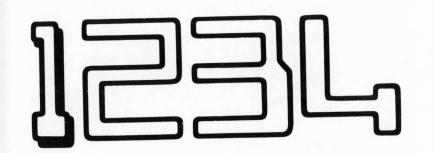

FROM A JOURNAL: 8/10/74, LAKE SUPERIOR

I see clouds, an arc of clouds bound together into one. And sometimes a sea gull will suddenly flip into view as if the clouds had chipped off a bit of themselves and twisted it into a sea gull. The clouds are very light, opalescent; not dark, not thin, just *that*; a lovely Minnesota thatness located a few inches above the head and stretching all the way to the horizon over the lake.

And inside, a hunger, a wonderful emptiness that loves its growling hunger. Each morning it returns, a miracle of hunger for the world, loving its lightness in the face of the world's fullness, the gorged physicalness of things, the hundreds of purple-tipped weeds crammed along the bank, their tips swinging wildly in the thickness of the wind, so gorged and full and heavy with dance and height and depth and inside this lightness, faintness almost, this hunger which is *always hunger*, which will never fill and is not meant to fill—permanent hunger.

And then I think of the other hunger. The hunger of distended bellies. I can't help it, I want to be light and swing in my lightness, but that other hunger strikes me full in the face, invades my lightness, firm and heavy like that strange man in Duluth yesterday standing on the corner, rubber boots in the middle of summer, huge galoshes and black beard, at least fifty, long gray coat flapping around him and I thought of the Mandelstams, the long flapping coats given them so they could survive the winter. And the luxury of an egg, a single egg which luckily, by the purest chance, they happened to have and Nadya was able to give it to Osip—that was the first time he was arrested, the time he survived. And Hernandez slowly dying in prison in Spain, writing that incredible poem to an onion, the fullness of the onion, as he died of hunger, starved into TB by Franco with his fat belly draped in silk sashes.

And, yes, I tremble in my emptiness. I do not carry my lightness lightly. It is a heavy lightness, it is carried with the heartbreaking lightness of a feather, for I have been blown by an arbitrary wind into this cabin by this lake which makes so much lightness possible. This feather blown here by money, so simple: money . . . which never gets into poems except by preaching; only Ignatow has stood looking at money in poems, has stood with awe in the face of its power, its abstract cruelty which with an absent flick of its heavy wrists has blown me here, to this calm, this open-ended tunnel of light facing onto waves and sea gulls and has blown Elizabeth into the factory and the guy who makes bags all day for $2.50 an hour and I worry if I smoke my pipe too much while he worries will his hands be too sore to hold a pen . . .

I will not create a false link between these hungers, between the single human tear on the face of the betrayed and humiliated man in Atlanta and the whole body of water in this huge lake with its waves and sea gulls, for there is no link; the tear on the cheek of the man in Atlanta weighs exactly the same as all the water in this Minnesota lake. They are separate, like separate moons, each with its own gravity, each pulling at me, independent, their existences separate and pulling each from its own orbit, pulling on me and I cannot deny either of them, though each pulls so relentlessly, each would have me for its own, each would shape my tides to its own pull and each does.

But even within me, even within this single coherent body which is able to thread a lace through the eye of a shoe, even in the miraculousness of such a body there is no link between the two tides, no way they connect into one smooth beach, and there is no way to ever finish the poem of these two existences and all other existences. The poems of our torn lives go on and on and somewhere inside us we know that the tides will keep tearing at us, keep feeding off us because we are human and the rhythms of the world invade us from all directions at once and always will and to say anything else is a lie, a beautiful lie with a tide all its own which is also inside me, pulling me constantly to speak of "loose ends" and "hidden connections" and that is there, too, with its own compelling weight, sending out its feelers, too. Love, the love of uncovering one*denial after another, the joy in sadness and in fear, the definite joy in surviving: Solzhenitsyn, Mandelstam, Hernandez . . .

they speak from the very last corner of existence, the ledge that looks out over the lake, the last spit of earth where the small wind-stunted pine grows and there is no coherence, but a noticing so deep it brings a joy stronger even than the longing for wholeness.

LOST WORKER ROOTED IN THE WORLD

Huge wooden loom;
foreboding, like an altar.
Behind it sits a man in gray cap and gray shirt
working the foot pedal, face gone vacant in the intricacy of his task,
so repetitive and detailed, so lulling in its precise rhythm.
It is a wooden labyrinth with a man at one end and an unlit lantern at
    the other.
Nearby is the table with four thickly glazed brown bottles.
one on its side like an anchor.
A worker's room,
its looms and bottles like gnarled roots growing around the man
who works in the hollow space at its center.

The orphan is dark, too;
small and brown.
when I try to carry her she holds back,
then takes my hand and guides me into a gray office building.
We see my father.
He is happy, brisk
as he steps off the escalator,
so unlike the man at the loom who looks as if he will never wake,
as if the cloth will never arrive at its fullness
in the world of endlessly spinning thread.
My father leads us to the girl's foster mother,
beautiful behind the bank of telephones
where she connects men who are happy in their decisions,
their moving of grain from one end of the world to the other.

The silver escalator hums in the background.
It is going down.
I step on and grab hold of the railing.
I am going to the man in the gray cap endlessly working his loom.
I need to see the girl's real father one more time
who lives and works in a job with no future,
as if he had no child.

AT THE LAUNDROMAT

I sat at the very end of the laundromat,
so old there wasn't even Muzak, no shiny pink washing machines,
the ceiling full of peeling paint like a book with its pages burned.
My eyes felt thick, my sight poured out of me in columns, focused,
I *saw*, say "saw" slowly three times and you will feel the odd heft of
this vision:
saw, saw, saw,
the way I felt my third night out of prison when we walked through a
  stubble field
to the river I had never seen by daylight and sat there
in the cool October night, the river below us down a steep bank,
sat there watching the blackness for many minutes,
felt the black motion of my own heavy body for the first time in ten
  months
and in that laundromat it came again, everything there
heavy with use, the huge ceiling fan, black, encrusted with dirt, each
  blade thick with it
and at the other end the short man in the green shirt who ran the place,
one of those puke green knit shirts buttoned to the top,
he sorted laundry, slowly, very slowly, taking each piece out of the
  dryers,
shaking it once, holding it to the light, shaking it again,
then (if it were coat or shirt) lifting it to his nose
and smelling the armpits, smelling each one carefully
and finally hanging them in a long row ready for pickup.

It was late, almost 10 P.M., and he called out to another laundromat.
At first he seemed happy and then angry as he complained bitterly,
how they hadn't cleaned the machines,
how he would shake them up good soon, how they listened to the
  radio—
no more radios!—it was quarter to ten and they still had time to do the
  windows.

My whole body then was with his body, I felt the rising anger in us
      both,
heavy, weighted, each in our clumsy bodies. I could feel
the pull of him, as if dragging me across the dance floor,
teaching me a new step at dancing class, no
future, no future, our hands sunk to the elbows in soap,
twisting the shirts into rags, sinking the rags one by one,
cleaning the dry gains of soap off the table tops one last time,
removing the thumb prints from the plate glass,
pulling back the tab on the cash register, making the room black.

THE HISTORY OF ROSES

7 A.M., first frost, the nurse who works all night
walks home, feet splayed gingerly in two directions.
Last night the old man who sells papers by day and flowers by night
sold us roses, five for a dollar. And the world
sways a little on its stem at how people have to shuffle
to survive.

And now there are roses on your desk, concentrated slices of dawn,
darkened, folded into layers, veined and bunched together,
coil of soft petals above the delicate green leaves.
And the history of roses is the history of the work whistle,
the florist for whom holidays are a nightmare,
whose children are asleep by the time he's home Christmas Eve,
who stands alone in the kitchen he remodeled and eats a dish of ice
        cream
before he goes to bed: he is still young when his first heart attack
        comes.

There is no end to the history of roses, to blooming and quiet,
to what withers and returns. All knowledge hurts:
and when we walk out of a theater and buy roses
there have to be tears and oceans and blind trust
in the clot of a dark red substance on the end of a cut stem.

ONE REASON I WENT TO PRISON

A boat gathers you in,
fools you by rocking gently,
makes you feel you're safe
as the waves gently lap
at the prow. When it
goes down, women and children
escape first, the men
work together as heroes.
Then, the time comes,
it's you and your father,
sink or swim, neither
can swim without the other,
each sinks separately
going his own direction
down and down and down.
Yet something solid finally
grabs your ankles, sand
under you, push up, the surface
is not so far away, your
father is not dead either
even says
"He must be brave."
It was the only chance
I had to show you I could
make it alone, over my head.
If I had known we'd go together,
even to the bottom of my own grief,
maybe, then, it would have been
unnecessary to prove myself
your enemy.

TO WHOEVER HAS TO WORK
MY JOB IN PRISON

At lunch you can sit with your friends
and laugh at your boss. Or, perhaps
you are beyond that, into the new
territory of ridicule and bitterness,
I know for sure you must hate
by now the picture of the first thirty presidents
on your left and the barred windows
on your right. Behind you the filing cabinets
and beyond them the bathroom
where at least you can masturbate in peace
to the truth, violence, or tiredness
you find deepest in your heart.

TERRY

Terry by his window at dawn. He's been in prison
so long he's got a corner bunk
with *two* windows. He sits
with his back against the footlocker,
feet on his bed, coffee cup in hand,
eyes wide open. One hand
goes to his bald head. Serious,
another day begun.

Terry happy does a jig, dancing
down the hallways where no man
danced before. Or, giving Tony
a "birthday cake"—a cupcake
with matches for candles.
Or, passing Terry in the yard as he jogs,
sweat dripping off his chin, tired,
no words, only time for one weak false-toothed grin.

Terry caught up in the streets,
trying to figure his sister-in-law
or the crazy girl who wanted him to beat her
and how when he gets out he'll
just get on a bicycle, travel up and down the coast,
work when he has to, meditate,
get stoned and make love as much as possible.
And stay away from that money thing.

Next month he goes up for parole,
has a chance since this is his first fall.

(January 1971)

RESOLUTIONS

This year I'll be a hair shirt in reverse,
teeth on fruit and a tongue in the secret places,
a psalm in the face of my enemies,
the nail that works loose from every theory,
two steps toward whatever moves,
a cool basement for my goat to play in,
and this year I'll take ten fingers
and write slowly of the prisons,
no sadness will be spared,
no cell forgotten, no guard
will believe he is human
and every day I'll remember
the length of each convict's body.
It is because *they* are doing more than time
that *I* can turn my self-hate on its head
and remember the new year is everywhere
and fuck up on occasion
and let the world fuck up
and join my friends in the tunnels
where in spite of everything
Terry danced a jig once and I watched
and I think I'll bathe in the sea
and let no more than a little salt water
separate Terry and me.

LETTER TO MARY

for Grish, Terry, Grant & the others

At dinner there was a woman crazy for airports
but I couldn't help her: I tried to be runways and waiting rooms
                    and businessmen in a hurry,
it just didn't work.
So I argued with a professor instead and drank lots of wine
                    and ate a delightful Italian soup
                    with a lemon taste like fingers taste
                    if you suck on them a long time
and then later I talked with some women (you were there in
                    those funny socks and with that book
                    full of suicide which started this
                    all off)
and leapt into my midnight life, joined by my faithful kitten,
                    Federal Time,
the sort you do forever in a joint like Marion or Lewisburg
                    or Leavenworth.
Federal Time is upset because I won't go to bed, but I can't
                    because of this letter to my right-now
                    favorite person, Mary Hilmer,
because of all these friends who are in
lonesome places, though asleep probably or maybe just getting
                    up to work in the kitchen
and one thing they all know for sure, which is you, Mary,
                    won't be there this dawn and the other
                    dawns that keep sauntering up and down,
                    up and down, so as to make your head
                    spin and your heart ache for just one
                    dawn without loudspeakers and without
                    all those gray footlockers, without
                    things labeled "personal possessions."
So, on or about the day of Oct. 23, 1971, I celebrated one year
                    away from that place

and my new kitten, one Federal Time by name, began to cotton
                    to me a bit and put his head on
                    my wrist and sleep.

And in that sleep I see many things, but most of all one
                    moonless night in Greece before the
                    revolution of the testicle beaters
on the small island of Tinos frequented only by seedy French
                    tourists and German pharmacists
on a narrow beach road very late there stood a windmill and
                    inside it a light and a head in the
                    gleam of the light bent over something
                    and for the gleam on the hair of the head
I wept because I was lonely and had not met the men I came
                    to love in prison and was not yet
                    enchanted by a pair of crazy socks
                    and the earnest suicide of a young
                    poet
and had not yet felt the head of a small animal rest on
                    the pulse of my wrist and so could
                    not possibly be this not happiness,
                    not sadness of now, because I was twenty-one and
                    full of self-pity because the man in
                    the windmill did not speak my language
                    (nor I his)
and this poem, going on now these seven years, never quite
                    at home in my body until this moment
                    when it all appeared at once and led
                    me by the hand for an hour and whispered
                    such things in my ear that I give them
                    to you like mist, not to be seen through
                    but accepted and shared for the space
                    of this moment.

ATTICA

Now that the deaths have come in
we watch debates.
Now that the men are dead
comfortable conference chairs will have to be built.
Smooth-topped tables will have to replace
live bodies. Sharpened pencils will have to do
instead of breath. Paragraphs of the proper length
and correct weightiness. I know you'll leave this poem
the man you were when you came. You'll make
no "unreasonable" demands, will not seek
freedom in a third-world country, will not
die and will not bother to read the committee reports
and you will be right. But you will be right
to no purpose, no better than a report yourself
and with nowhere to take your anger
as the dead men had no place to take theirs.

There can be no revolution without the grave.
Now the Fascists have the day, but life underneath
goes on: Allende, Neruda, the tree out my window
rootless, its leaves going yellow, brown . . .

but in its season: the cracked husk brings its own kind of luck.
In the private fields of grief I am only half a life
and the crow repeats itself endlessly like tears of self-pity.
In the real fields—owned by no one—life goes on:
deep on the ground grief turns to anger and the hay
stands in the barn. We widows cut our hair
and leave the strands to the future: long bundles of grief
which you must not be afraid to eat.

OLD MAN IN MICHIGAN

for Ed

Cold. Sky clouded over. Even the asparagus field
half-buried in snow. Up at the farmhouse
the old man is happy to be retired.
In the forties he found himself
a "small-time farmer" though his father
and grandfather before him never had
to see themselves that way.
Forced into the factory, his union
was stolen, the men swayed by free beer
and redbaiting. At its worst
he was hung in effigy as a Communist
from the old bridge, near the Hagar schoolhouse.

Ed likes himself as an old man.
"At my age you don't regret much."
Jake comes over, the two of them
drink brandy and reminisce. Usually
it is Jake who does the talking.
The old man laughs and pours
the brandy. They remember the Wobblies
who hit the hobo jungles
with slogans and Chaucer.
"They had the spirit, but they
never stuck around to organize.
When they moved on, the locals
broke up." Jake is mad as he remembers.
Ed puts his hand to his face,
nothing confused in the gesture,
but sixty-five, tired out.

Every day with his two dogs, he goes
down by the dam and over to his brother's place,
the one who collected the guns when the government
came to bulldoze the cherry trees. "Now,
an apple or a pear tree, why it don't
make that much difference. But,
you plant a cherry tree as a young man
and you hate to see it go."

In the book *Oriental Mythologies*
we hear of four hundred people getting happily
buried alive for the love of a king.
This book has so many strange stories of happy men
who carry terrifying illusions as though they were butterflies
which one honors by not touching.

Everywhere I look I see my imperfect friends
and our unhappy acknowledgment of truth after truth,
as if we were elevators
believing we are going up quickly, quickly.

6/8/72

for Adrienne Rich

You sleep through Nazi dreams, my brother.
Did you think living in the country would stop the nightmares,
could stop the history tanks?
Did you think unspoiled farm hogs could stomp out Adrienne's truth:
history keeps coming. You are my brother,
but I can't keep it from you, not even from you.
The beautiful countryside is not a museum:
I don't mean the war of the ants or natural battles,
but what the corporations have planned for the cities
reaches out patiently to the fields, the quarries, the sheds, the
        horseshoe pits.
You are delicate, you meditate and are often silent,
but they are subtle. Your silence counts for nothing,
your meditation puts you quietly at their side.
But we are brothers. I know your silence has a trapdoor,
we meet beneath it at night.
You massage my blunt muscles,
my stiff neck. How gently you relax me.
In your arms there is mercy and a clear space,
in your bed we form a half-shell, an arch
over the open graves.

COMING BACK FOR HELP

for Thomas McGrath

We have all these poems about darkness and hidden water,
sad attempts to take us away from ourselves,
to find the boats
without captains that will return us to the sea,
will float us into perfection,
perfect sailors of the unconscious.
Is solitude so bleak?
Do we become perfect as we strip our lives of affection,
is snow blindness the final absolution?

It is winter now in St. Paul. I am alone,
I love my teacup with its bird under the curved flower,
the way sunlight illumines the little clouds of dust-hair in my room
and in the evening the sound of a radio floats in from down the street,
the voice of the announcer sad in its forced intensity.

Voice,
they would give you a funeral at sea,
but you'll come back,
message scribbled in a bottle,
crying for help
because we always do,
no matter how we long
to finger
the stone harp of purity
in the coldest water
of the most inhuman ocean.

PEACE AND RESISTANCE

All over this city I have found
Friday night; in some
apartments parties, in others
solitary cats in darkened windows.
Some places doors slam,
in others records play.
I crossed a road
and got to the other side,
I came in a room
where the bathroom light
was on. I shouted,
"Is anybody home!"
And, there I was,
willing to say it,
yes, peace,
peace and resistance
bless your happy home.

AFTER THE REVOLUTION: MUSIC

for Meridel Le Sueur

1

The cold egg of the snow cracks open,
broadens into chunks of fog.
10 A.M. and the street corner is invisible.
I turn on the electric heater, listen to Casals,
watch the branches like thin asparagus stalks
shrouded and growing under water.
Something lives here bigger than my skin,
larger even than the old man Pablo bent over his bow,
the old man Pablo brushing his quick strokes on paper,
the old man Pablo writing his last poem from a hospital bed.
Three Pablos dissolve into the tiger-rubbing fog,
yellow body ringed with black
that stalks the world's trembling seams.
The three of them move into the far distance.
This is the terrifying spring, shimmer of fog-breath,
huge muscles rippling against the tree.

At the trial they are talking about death.
The old Indians have faces that crease in all directions,
crisscrossed patches of flesh, long black hair.
Hundreds are indicted.
The young prosecutor wears a sweater under his jacket to keep off the
    chill.
And the deaths at Wounded Knee hover somewhere in that dark tiger—
    stalking fog.
Nothing is lost,
nothing disappears. The murders dissolve and then re-form into
    something new
in the distance where the tiger winds around the tree.

2

Night now.

Quarter moon behind trees.

Down the block the yellow-lemon light that is always there.

At sunset the last of the fog was caught, pink, like a glaze separated
      from its pot.

Today in Spain two anarchists from the mountains garroted:

a leather collar with a nail sticking out is placed around the neck and
      tightened.

The moon clears the trees now and hangs free in the sky, bodiless.

3

Three days ago I bought a Zuni bracelet,

the first jewelry I have ever owned.

I thought about it a long time,

wore it around the shop and shook my wrist like a dancer trying on
      new shoes.

There are small pieces of turquoise and coral,

bits of the mastodon world like a speck caught in the eye.

Vision of the small, tears from another culture set in silver;

wrist streak, flesh bark.

The silver in the bracelet shivers in sunlight, glows in candlelight;

a white arc of music for the eye,

vibrations scattered like small campfires along the beach.

I see cello phosphorescence, curved fingers along the bow,

an old man's notations thrown back over his shoulder.

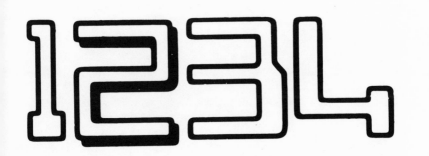

LONELINESS

1

They are so alone in the mist,
the two geese in the Japanese woodblock
that fly in front of the full moon.
One of them hunches his back for better flight
like a runner at the block, his wings arched to work full force.
The other one
glides; moves by some unseen power,
maybe the moon's pull shoots him along through the faint clinging mist
like a boat, oars up, drifts through seaweed.
And their claws!
Sharp, scaly, ready to drop
on some helplessness,
plummet through mist like pickaxes
detached from their hands.
They are alone in the world that supports wings,
the world of moon-shadows and thinning atmospheres.

2

My first night in Crete an old fisherman and I shared a bed.
"It's the custom."
Old broken pipe going, he looks at pictures in a magazine,
then puts it down. Sighs.
I look straight at him,
he puts his arms out, palms up, meaning:
"No language." Saying,
"I am at the river and must cross. Do you know of a boatman?"

WOLF

1

The wolf always comes at the last moment,
alone. He is never full,
you never can throw him enough bones.
When I see a wolf, even a photograph,
I shiver
as if I've been holding tears back a long time.
Something taut and frozen inside me wants to stretch on and on;
winter river, glint after glint stretched out under the sun.
Old oak bones that hang onto their trees,
clutched hand at the wolf's neck:
in the world of fur everything makes sense.

2

This is the wolf:
what is left when you've tried to throw everything away.
On the railroad bridge at Hennepin
sometimes I'll cry out "I'm so sad, I'm so sad"
and watch the grain elevators miles down the tracks
and in the middle between the rails
the grass is black like vertical threads of coal.
On the banks, old dead snow,
gray and mottled.

Part of him lives in the city
where people stand in record stores at midnight
and paw through the stacks,
their hands stumbling, confused,
abandoned in a strange street,
expected to make their way . . .

3

To find the wolf
look at anything wary, anything falling down.
That old woman on West Seventh
directing traffic with a torn branch,
the tree all twisted from growing between apartment houses.
Or the time I lifted the garbage can lid
finding the flowers
from when the baby downstairs died,
turned on their side in the bottom of the can;
bright yellow, still growing in the darkness
like hair on a corpse, or a tear
falling down the cheek of a paralyzed man.

BRACED AGAINST WEIGHTLESSNESS

What is the slow curve of an airplane at night,
if not the hope of some further silence:
seats empty, the glow of the instrument panel gone out,
landing lights blank against a thinning atmosphere.
The captain, arms folded, stares up at the unused oxygen mask.
The plane picks up speed, the dark windows look out on miles of
      unused light years
and far below an earth disappears, an old curve of light pulling back,
gives up its salty claims, its blanket of oxygen, its heavy minerals
fly away like sand. A fine dry ice forms on the wing.
The captain stands awkwardly in the small space of the cockpit,
braced against his own weightlessness.
If only his old glove of an earth could come with him,
then he would not be afraid. If only death were a department store
or a short walk to the mailbox. But the plane goes on,
two wings in a great emptiness carrying a captain
who on a sudden impulse lowers the landing gear,
but the stubby wheels might as well be stars
they are so silent and useless. He does not even bother to sit down,
but peers out the window where the shadow would have been.

IN THE FORMAL GARDEN

The old man sits apart from the others.
One of them, the tall woman whose hair points straight ahead as
    intently as her eyes,
is commissioned to do a portrait. She has him in profile.
He looks straight ahead into the late afternoon sun.
He has arranged his gold collection before him in a sort of altar.
He faces the discs, barely aware of the people. As the coins catch
the late afternoon sun a yellow halo forms around them.
He has never seen anything so lovely and he has been rich a very long
    time.
He calls his wife over for a look, but by the time she has walked
the few feet to his side the sun has shifted and the coins look old and
    dirty
like cornhusks left in the fields through winter.
He is embarrassed he bothered her and doesn't know what to say.
The others talk among themselves. He is annoyed.
The portrait is taking a long time. The artist's hair points straight ahead
and throws shadows like spikes over the rich man's closely cropped grass.

ANNIE DRAWING

for Annie Hayes

When you draw, your hand curves in against your wrist
like a child hiding a small animal from her parents.
You sit in a straight-backed kitchen chair, thick board on your lap
and heavy boots on your feet, but your heels lifted as in ballet.
Your thick fingers curved inward jerk like sand crabs across the paper.

From the very first, your pen draws blood,
my forehead under your fingers is thick lines,
our eyes meet a moment and mine are transformed on the heavy paper
    into shadows.

We sit a few feet from each other like two dreams
about to enter the same tangled unconscious.
In my dream we are on a toboggan. I am afraid,
but you put your hands over mine and guide us.
It is almost dusk, the trees like ink drawings of skeletons.
I cannot see your dream, though its outlines swirl around me
fluid and demanding like a tide pulling me out, a beach disappearing
        beneath my feet.

WHERE THE DREAM ENDS

That little used-car lot. Only a few automobiles and trucks, a square of light bulbs above it. Why is it out here in the middle of nowhere? There should be an old cemetery on a hill like this or a small abandoned schoolhouse.

The family is almost in awe of the white Ford truck. The eldest son wipes and wipes the hood. Finally it is theirs! The mother has had a permanent recently. She wears tortoise-shell glasses that come to little points on the side of her face. She stands musing on the rise of the hill, looking at her son: "Well, if it all *does* finally come to an end I want to be with my family."

They all pile in the truck and move off quickly down the road. I am the only person left there, standing in the car lot at the end of a dream. They are not people of my class, I do not recognize where the car lot is, I am not the salesman.

THE NEW BODY

1

The old body strains to disappear.
Inside it is scooped out like the seatless canoes
Vikings laid their dead in.
The old tree of the canoe points upwards
toward the sky; oarless,
drifting into a thinner atmosphere.

What is it that holds back?
Familiar lassitude, fear of letting go—
like the half-empty bottle of wine
sitting for months on the kitchen shelf,
garbage piling up on the backstairs.
How afraid I was to go up to the famous man after his speech
and say, "Sir, I don't understand you.
I live alone in a boarding house.
I spend all my time reading Kant. Help me."

2

Yesterday I threw myself on the floor, trembling,
my skin shrunk over the knots of tightened muscles.
I drew the woolen shawl up over my body,
gasping for air as after orgasm
when the body is still streaming
toward its purified skin; but the moment passes,
buried in the split fruit of the vagina,
in the cove beyond the last tourist cabin
where we built the raft last summer,
working long after sunset, our bodies invisible to each other,

creating a third thing to carry us over water,
like the smell of leaves on your clothes
when you are a boy and have been playing in the huge piles all
      afternoon.
Little shreds of leaf-skin stick to your shirt
and when you go to bed that night your chest gives off a new smell.

3
We made love
and against the familiar boundary of your flesh
I felt my own body grow back;
a new shape, large enough to hold the trembling.
Something snapped,
like the deer we startled last year at Canby.
His leaps
were doors swinging open into new rooms.

I pull in air,
a man under water breathing through a hollow reed;
my skin like clear glass,
so new I almost forget it exists
and walk through it.
But something stops me.
I press against the invisible edges of my body
like a mime
pushing against the unreal walls of his prison cell.
What happens if the glass shatters,
if you leave the skin behind,
step into the fragrant bruise beyond . . .

FROM THE EDGE OF THE SHELL

When the river turns on itself
it makes shells. When it has had enough
of itself, wet and open and formed by banks
it turns on the bank that has gently contained it
and eats it, works its way in by sharp little picks.
The water of the river
makes shells, fragile and sharp, yet curved always into spirals,
at infinite pains to hide their emptiness.

They are amphibians. They stay there
as a man trying to make a decision
will pick his fingernails or run his hands through his hair;
and in his indecision become arresting and beautiful, like a deer at tree
      line
trying to decide whether to risk the forrest.

A shell gradually forms around such a man:
a moustache, or a distinctive walk or laugh.
Maybe he jogs precisely one mile a day
and all the while the shell becomes more and more delicate, fragile,
like winter on Lake Michigan which sends itself through the apple trees
until they are the most brittle of masks, until that awful stress
makes it utterly impossible to say whether the blossoms will ever come
      or the fruit or the windfall.

AT 7 A.M. WATCHING
THE CARS ON THE BRIDGE

Everybody's going to work. Well,
not me, I'm not
going to work.

TO THE READER

for Jack Litewka

The dunes here are small hills with lots of green weeds and old salt-whitened logs. The little cabin faces away from the ocean and from time to time I go outside and look. Sun, salt, and wind swirl around and through my body as if I were a skeleton or a scarecrow light as straw.

There is no one on this beach for miles. No other cabins, no road into the beach. Mountains and thick forests alternate for miles behind me.

If you have been in a place for years it fans out before you like branches on an old elm tree in winter. Late afternoon is best. By then my skin is thick with salt. The heavy sea air clings to my nostrils and pubic hair. My penis is heavy and rough-grained, warm in the last of the afternoon sunlight.

The Senoi in Malay tell their dreams over breakfast each morning. There has been no fighting there for two hundred years. If you dream you hurt someone, the next morning you must apologize and give him a gift—a new song or dance or a rhythm for his drum.

Today I fell down a well. I pushed further down and came out the other side clear across the country to this place in this cabin by the ocean. Now I am awake in St. Paul where I cannot see you and do not know you, just as I have never seen my cabin at the ocean. It is our place now, yours and mine.

HOW TO CLOSE THE GREAT DISTANCE
BETWEEN PEOPLE

Do it over coffee,
like fish that appear to be talking,
but are really eating to stay alive.

DOORS

for Madeline

For a long time I tried to open the door by reading books about doors, going into the matter of wood and so on. I forgot about the *real* door. I lived in a new world in which "door" had to be put in quotes because no one knew what it was, though a few remembered them from childhood.

Once I locked a friend of mine in a bathroom and wouldn't let him out until I knew he was good and angry. If he wouldn't love me, I at least wanted the strongest bond possible.

Whenever I read a poem in which doors appear I am happy. Tranströmer has so many doors he is a regular hotel of the spirit: no matter what your room number, or what floor you are on, when you put the key in (and each key is different), turn the lock and open up, you enter—not your own room—but "the room for everyone." We stand there, brushing snowflakes off our coats and making small talk, but really, we're happy to finally be together. We all have copies of Tranströmer's poems about doors and we eagerly compare them and begin the job of translating into each other's languages.

Everything adds up. That's why we have hands that open into fingers and not claws. That's why we are bodies and not cans of vegetables. To get through doors, to hold them open for others, to take them off their hinges and use them for beds. When I was a kid I made a raft out of a door and a crippled kid helped.

Think of it! And even without doors one gets along, falls in love, picks up where he left off. Didn't Virginia Woolf write about doors, didn't everyone I love come walking through a door into this room? My skin prickled, my body went taut with pleasure because everything I need is here, as conscious of me as I am of everything.

Didn't Wendy, didn't Keith and Dave and all the people I love, didn't they find their way here, even though I used to throw snowballs at cars and mistreat my sister?

SUNSET

1

The sun spins off into its last corner
down by the steel webbing that supports water towers,
down every stalk, into the stones with their layers of blackness,
giving breath to dust and blood to loneliness.

A kite string breaks,
the kite floats like a detached wing, single wing-tip,
through the narrowing band of light, high
over Applebaum's neon sign,
away into the valley, over the curve of the small houses in the Czech
    neighborhood.

All falls down.
Light glitters along the frozen edges of the turnpike.
Chromatic dismembering,
totally alone in the changing scales of light
like a small boy standing in the dusk of his parents' bedroom.
Downstairs the baby sitter watches TV. The boy stands by his father's
    bureau
and sees the familiar neighborhood go dark, sees the trees
on Reising's hill, their branches like huge nests in the last light.

2

Children in the dusk.
The last line of carelessness,
jump ropes cutting a floating erratic arc in the purple sky.
Their voices rise,
human voice mist, a silver casualness
thrown back into the dark.

Sadness,
because there are no questions to ask,
because all desires are coded into every part of the sky,
like walking through your own breath,
the slow life-pulse of changing light,
air passing in and out of your lungs, moving through the thinning
      world.

3

What hides behind the dusk?
Light-sluice for another world,
down there at the end of the west-facing block,
only orange shards point the way, cairns on the journey
to the looming mountains, the blackness beyond tree line,
larger than an open mouth, as large as the turtle's journey
as he drags through the wet sand to the river.

The fading light is inside you.
All the times you have been alone rise from the blood,
the orange wisps of solitude swirling around inside;
light lifts off the earth, finished;
everything finished.

A lone swing in the park.
Cold metal chains and a wooden seat.
The skin listens for its forests
as your feet scrape along the scooped-out dust under you.
You push up and out in the metal-squeaking dusk,
farther and farther out, parallel with the tops of trees.
You long for something friendly,
peer into the swinging disappearing earth
like a duck flying north
toward the long-absent marsh, the swerve back into earth waters.

TWO FLUTE SONGS

1

I want to become thin as a flute song
which goes into the delicate inner ear
and coils there, holding in balance the lives
of everyone I love.

2

It's late and the furnace goes full blast
filling the room like a good joke.
I read aloud, pausing for rain.
If my pipe were alive
I could not hold it more lovingly.
Soon, I will make green tea
and pray that the flute song I barely hear
is not a signal for dawn
and is not a record, nor an answer
to any questions I might pose it.

TRAPPED

1

I wake into a 3 A.M. stillness so complete
my head starts to spin inside it,
a cat stuffed in an airtight bag tied to an exhaust pipe.
Eyes closed,
my body rocks beyond control,
muscles and brain wanting to fall back again into the long alley of sleep.
My fear grows,
that the volley of nerve endings will misfire again and again,
that the body will float out on the black 3 A.M. lake before it is
　　　noticed.
Everyone on shore motions
for the young boy to paddle with his hands.
He is confused; drifts farther and farther out
on the yellow plastic raft. He waves back at them,
wants to be polite;
but the idiot life in deep water calls him . . .

2

And now, all these years later,
the caws of the sea gulls are sad to me
because the whine of the kitten inside them
has no wings, can find no lake to swoop over,
has let its claws be bitten down to fingernails.
Father, I cannot find the wind
that would float me silently to your side.
Your thin legs, soft belly, curved breasts:
are all fathers so strange when they sit on the toilet?
Your body behind the opaque door of the shower,
steam on the mirror,
water breaking against your heavy body.

When I was in prison we hugged.
You wore an expensive gray suit,
I, sharp-creased visiting-room browns.
Under the clothes our bellies rubbed
before we sat on the orange chairs in front of the guards.

I jogged in that place,
imagined myself a Viet Cong
on the Ho Chi Minh Trail.
Father Ho wrote poetry.
In *Life* it said his house had no bodyguards.
So many years in prison
and no visiting hours to see his son.
Did he have a son? I have a father.
You walked in the river and freed a duck.
It was I who handed you the net.
The secret is in our bellies
touching under the eyes of the guards.

3

There is so much I can't see yet,
this sense of the trees giving secret commands
I can't quite make out.
I crawl like a root sucker
in the mud along the north side of the hill
among the crumpled-up cigarette packs,
sodden and trampled; the beer cans
caked with dirt, empty, kicked down
from the crown of the hill,
here to the scraggly bushes.

We drink wine,
sleep in the sun and look at the blue smear of the river far beneath us.
Later, I walk past the edge of town,
out along a country road where redwing blackbirds live.
An old man is putting in a garden.
He has gone in for lunch
and planted one glove each on two sticks of his picket fence
and his hat on a third.
My hands are balled into fists, gripping their fear;
like the woman in the blue coat
walking so purposively,
her hands pointed straight out before her,
as if she were blind,
stumbling through the thickets of air.

Back in the city spring multiplies in a drunkenness of mud and water:
old dog shit melting into formless brown pools,
the houses with high fences like barbed wire,
the small attic window where there is always the sound of typing,
sudden whine of a siren turning into a shriek,
the mother who shouts, "OK, fifteen minutes!"
the mother who shouts, "Now!"
The top of my head wants to lift off,
join the box kite with its frayed edges
caught in the web of branches.
Sometimes five senses are not enough,
not enough cups to catch the rain,
the bodiless voices from open windows,
wind shifts,
new grass cracking open the dead earth.

4

Walking the prison yard on the first spring night
Doug said, "Remember street lights,
how they cast a shadow?"
We looked out past the old wooden gun tower
to the Missouri fields
ploughed into blackness; and there too, the redwing blackbirds
flinging themselves against the last light
beyond the prison glare,
almost brushing the fields
as if they were a second, wing-tipped, horizon,
moving so fast as to be barely visible.

We walked in an invocation of street lights
that lit up Doug's freckled face,
that took his chewed-down fingernails into a trembling joy for his own
        past twilights.
This is the human wilderness beyond the body's last border
where the old man puts on his garden gloves again to grow fruit in the
        prison, the world.

CHILDHOOD

From the deep well to the stare of the hypnotist,
from calf-bound books to sherry in the marble.
from the glance that absolves you, to the low voice of an apologetic
     aunt,
from stunt to stunt in the childhood of met needs,
and back again, back again, back again,
the bob in the river, a turtle with no taste for the bottom—
patience in its red cork like a doctor on the stairs late at night.
And at 7 A.M. a bell in the black street warning,
"The Catholics are coming! The Catholics are coming!"

Confused dreams of the sleeper: a drunken father takes his daughter to
     the tavern.
his friends leer, he leers, "My God, you're beautiful, beautiful . . ."
And the daughter remembers naming the piles of leaves *Des Moines,
     Chicago,*
jumping in them—spectacular comets of childhood geography,
to name the destruction, to enter the port of fallen leaves,
to misuse the absence of parents by spectacular leaps.

And meanwhile the seal sleeps like an empty letterhead,
but there are sirens and barking dogs and a dough that rises in the east
where the sea meets the city in a rootedness of trees,
tears of adolescent amphibians seek a third way:
the time of the duck under the railroad bridge and the precision of the
     small boy,
alphabet stuffed in his pocket, packing his handkerchief full of marbles
     to run away . . .

THROUGH THE FEAR NET

1

I miss the thin line of trees in my parents' backyard,
the hedge that separated me from the street.
One Saturday, hitting a golf ball against the clothes post,
deep in some victory fantasy,
two Black kids came running through the bushes.
They bullied me, threw me to the ground,
said they'd come back to kill me.
As they disappeared back through the bushes
I lay there crying in the grass,
terrified, as later I would pound the kitchen table,
cry out against friends afraid of burning draft cards,
call them evil
because my own fear was so great.

My father said I should fight back,
give the bullies a taste of their own medicine.
This made sense.
I set up a punching bag in the basement of our house.
About this time my fantasies began,
that a tunnel connected the whole house,
a secret panel in the basement let me in:
I could listen to everything my parents whispered about me
by crawling through the skin of the house,
secret loneliness web, hidden connection,
blood network, sniffer and digger of roots.
That was the summer my father said,
"Why don't you have any friends?"

Once I walked beyond the last housing development,
cheap wood tacked to cheap wood,
strips of concrete like open wounds at their bases

and in the dusk beyond the last fragile street light
I felt my own thick bark peel away
and watched the gray river ripple past me,
round the small clump of trees and scraggly bushes.
The air itself grew thick and gray, thin atmosphere of dusk water.
I knelt there on the grass, faced the river and prayed,
defenseless in my skin. I cried.

2

Old man, I see you in the park,
head dwarfed under your racing cap;
you lean forward slightly and stare
at the valley beneath you, the huge hills in the distance
that blot out the sky like giant waves.
How can you sit in the cold so long,
motionlessly? What your stillness means to me
means nothing to you. I am still so pale.
You sit erect, without strain, on the cold concrete of the bench.
I want to go back to the tears,
to the tunnel,
to the web of secrets,
even the fears and humiliations.
But this time with you,
old weather vane held together by flesh,
I want to sail with you.
In this water, sorrow is just a fin-slash,
one more dolphin lifting for a moment out of the ocean,
one more arrowhead buried in the earth,
chipped bone of human need
separated finally from its purpose,
mislaid spoke of the earth wheel
spinning free at last in the inhuman center of gravity.

SECRETS

for my mother on her birthday

Somewhere at this very moment someone is eating peanut butter right out of the jar! He is alone and the television is off. His mother has no idea what he is doing. It is his secret. Very far away a dog barks, a horn honks. The day his grandmother died he had a crazy desire to laugh and yet he was very sad. You don't tell your mother your secrets for fear she won't love you.

SO WHAT IF IT TAKES FOREVER!

for my father

1

I'll be the light I need in early morning
and the stone foundations, damp so long they're brown
and the skinny drainpipe, rusted, leading from the lip of the roof
to the concrete funnel to the street
and I'll be the long letter from a good friend, three pages single-spaced,
and the tobacco so good it was created in London for the Gentlemen of
     St. James
and all those things a kitten loves: ribbons, ping-pong balls, gum
     wrappers, warm milk
and more, I'll be more, the hours of meditation, the tedium of sitting,
the irresistible urge to snooze, to slip into unconscious alligator
     breathing, sunning in the swamp
and I'll have to be the jerk back into waking, the guilty grunt
and then the hours of nothing, blackness, waiting,
especially the waiting . . . for what?

2

In prison you wait
for 6 A.M. loud-speaker,
for breakfast you wait
for your shoelaces to wither,
for work call, for the long walk
down the tunnel, waiting
for the spastic director
of the "learning center"
to stutter, "h-h-h-h-ello."
you wait all during work
for the 4 P.M. count,
then stand in line and wait
for mainline, then again
in the dining hall,

you wait and listen to Muzak,
you forget your body,
what use is it here?
Your eyes, literally,
cannot stay open
hours on your bunk
under the blankets
hand on crotch,
everything empty,
waiting for lights out,
waiting for the big
nothing blizzard,
for the Snowman Stare,
for the White Hour
in which nothing appears

3

Climbing Flattop with my father, three summers ago,
"The smallest mountain in Colorado." according to my sister.
At first it was easy,
walking along the winding ridges that looked out
over endless miles of pine and glacier lakes.
We could see so far the air actually changed colors!
As we went up, trees changed to shrubs, we talked less,
concentrated on one last ridge we thought we had to get around to be
    there
and then discovered how far there was to go.
A half-mile cone stood before us, all rock, marked only by stone cairns
    to show the trail,
how it snaked up through the thin air
to more bare rock and a trail book to sign. Big deal.
My father's breathing so heavy he had to stop every few feet,
we moved on anyway, pausing often never speaking,

listening to ourselves breathe, ignoring the scenery,
stunned into silence, like riding waves or sticking your head out a
    speeding car.
Numbed already, then a wind came up and we put our jackets on,
I should loud as I could "Yaieee!"
and my father did a feeble two-step
and let the wind billow out his jacket.
We took our time, the long pauses grew longer
until finally we could not put off the triumph any longer
and we reached the top.

BEYOND THE WINDOW

1 A.M. radio saxophone and outside a street light on the telephone
    pole—
small white glow above the wires makes the wood look old
like hands in soapsuds—part of my mind already sorting out the day,
but the rest moves out along the two thin wires into darkness.
My father pausing in my room, says nothing, silence trailing off
into words about the weather—all that sadness crouching outside my
    boyhood window . . .
Black night and I regret nothing, Father!
Your shadow falling into the larger blackness
like a cup of wine thrown back into the bottle.

THE OLDEST SON

In the cellar the body full of eyes floats to the surface,
breasts rise up from the ulcerated stomach
and orange pine cones rub against the ridges of the thighs.
That night the son crawls down his rope ladder made from sheets
to the basement. The violet forest in his chest
guides the way. Mother tucks in the light,
father rolls over on his death and is sweetly asleep.
Sparks fly out of the urns of resentment
and the old maid's ferns give off a dank smell.
The son's scrotum scratches feebly against the basement walls.
The thing in the stomach howls like a dog.
Roots take hold.

A man pushes his way out of the basement.
Slits like gills have formed along his ribs.
Tears drip out over his buttocks and penis.
When he marries, his wife's fingers grow smooth,
then cracked from the saltiness. It is a deep secret between them.
They have no children.

HOW THE BOY WENT DOWN AND CAME UP

The birchbark canoe moves slowly, one oar, the white of the birchbark flashing in and out of the blue white horizon. Far away, on the west coast, the old lighthouse still works, the huge lens—ground in Paris—sends out its signal every twelve seconds. To the child in the birchbark canoe it flashes like the light of the firefly on a distant hill, that hill of the night which creeps up so slowly, the other side of which is always invisible . . .

The boy is running away from the ancient statue. Months ago his parents left him there, said he had to sit at its foot and wait. But finally he thought he could hear the huge stones groan and he ran away in terror. He knew he was only a speck on the horizon, but still he paddled; his size did not matter, only the sound of the oar falling with a slosh into the water and then, whish, out again regular as a song. He invented a song:

> Oar, oar, where do you take me?
> Is there a home on the other side?

and the oar answered:

> slow, slow;
> slow, slow.

It was this way a long time and then the horizon split neatly in half and another canoe came toward him. At first he thought it was a gull it was so small and so far away. As it drew nearer the boy saw a man. When they were almost side by side the man stood and dived from his canoe. He sank like a large turtle which had only come up a moment for air. As soon as he was under water the oar became a divining rod and pulled him down very fast. The water was cold. He passed the man whose lungs had filled with water and was floating upward now. Suddenly the boy saw a cave and the oar carried him there. Now the water was only knee high and the boy stood up in the sand. He didn't need the oar anymore and he stood it on end against the cave wall. He walked slowly through the cave. As he walked it grew lighter and lighter. Finally he came to the end and walked out the other side. He saw his parents sleeping on a beach. Very quietly—so as not to wake them—he stepped over them and went into the forest beyond.

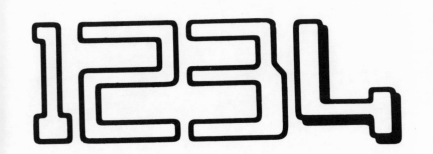

THE NEW MAN

1

Huge clumps of fur, damp, hang from the ceiling;
a dangle of wetness, like prickly cactus at night.
She stands erect, face hidden
behind the nearest clump. Her breath
rises and falls, the fur on the clump ripples along the edges of her
     mouth,
visible purring of the damp flesh fibers.

She wears clothes. Pants and purple shirt. Nothing moves
but the fur and her breasts under the shirt.
There are no words. Only the shirt's silken expansion,
the swelling of milk behind nipples, little pushings of milk,
glaucous life, an energy that moves with its own winds.

2

The mouse in the corner is barely visible behind his radishes,
paws sticky with radish juice, flecked white with radish flesh.
He's afraid
of the woman with fur for a face.
She is not listening. She has fur for ears.
She is not afraid. She stands motionless.
Still, he chews.

Behind the fur she sees a moon.
A full moon as if the fur were a night sky of branches.
She is tired of the mouse-husk, this nibbler of radishes
like an old man worrying his gums.
Is it for this she stood so still, for these lobeless ears,
for this collection of tics?
Her face still covered by fur she undoes her shirt, button by button.

The mouse watches.
There is no mouse-proverb to account for this.
If only I were stone!
If only this unbuttoning were a tiny hole
I could squeeze through.
Suddenly the mouse sees something silver in the air,
glint of breast-shadow,
nipple-mountain rising like a tail full of blood.

3
In the room of fur and radishes there is blood;
suckling,
a squeak that turns into a moan, belly-
stroke that leaves the mouse huskless,
human. Under his new green robe a penis rises.

3 A.M. / NEW MOON

The quarter moon
was newly risen and all yellow, dipped in the cream of its new birth
with no stars around it
and I was afraid because that quarter
will wax and wane free of us who live in its light and shadow
like tides pulled in and out by that swollen rock.
It hides and returns
and we hide and return.

Sometimes we have screamed and screamed,
hated each other and quit in disgust.
There is no secret.
You might as well forget it if you can and rest and do your daily work
until the next time. Stay away from the woman you love
until she is ready for you, until that moment when she shifts her
        position
ever so slightly as she reads and something is different again,
beginning to rise again in the east over the familiar human.

US

I cannot imagine loving an octopus,
but I love a woman who is coiled around
every direction. At once she grasps me *and* her loneliness,
forcing them together in the tentacles of her slippery strength.

She will not go down alone.
At the bottom of the sea her mother and father strangle her each night.
It is not a question of weapons or, "Will I dare it?"
I am alone too and desperately swim in every direction.

IN THE FORMLESS FUTURE

for Patricia

1

In the season of happiness, little comforts of orange bedspreads
and afternoon light splintering along a cracked windowpane.
We put our feet on the ledge and speak of leaving, separation.

We do not argue. This is not a fight.
We want to pull on the wishbone of solitude,
to sleep in the single bed again and extend
the circle of arms to include solitude:
like the full moon last night
behind its clouds;
transparent, a yellow
thin as tissue paper;
begin again,
layer behind cloudy layer.

2

A far place.
Some formless future
where Beethoven drifts off into deafness
and the last chords of a last quartet come together like strangers.

There are secret signs of recognition:
sadness overlapping sadness,
the strange hoots of mourning doves over the sounds of tires,
the cries of children.
          Lawn chairs set in a circle,
a little table with glasses on it.
Someone has just been here,
              someone will arrive soon . . .

FIRE

When it is too cold at night
sleep is dreamless, like a sky
very blue, very far away.
Warm animal truths
cannot stand it, cannot
come out to crease the mind
with wish presents
or terrors running free.
Deep, deep sky, empty
blue like a fingernail
with no history.

At such times the body
prints its dreams
in the skin, the muscles,
the posture.
You curl yourself,
a snail in the emptiness,
no longer human.
A helpless curl
laid out on the cold.

When you wake
your crotch is slightly damp,
an acrid smell,
lightning that has struck long ago,
its presence still lingering.
It reminds you,
"I have been somewhere."

You get up and stretch,
your body is still with you.
But your muscles are knotted
and hunched, trying
to crouch over a fire
somewhere in that cold.
You remember
wetness,
how the fur shivered
under your hand
long ago
before the moon split away
before women
before men.

THE SKY

The sky is like an animal we have never seen before
and will never see again. Suddenly it is here!
Our talk turns into whispers, then stops.
Nothing prepares us for this.
It is no butterfly, no animal at all
and remains silent as we become happy
or sad. Our lives no longer matter.
When it is blue or pink or red
we are nothing. For years beyond number it floats upwards.
There is nothing left to do but go
indoors and begin touching one another.

NEW BIRTH

I trust the bone at the back of your neck and your warm hair
matted and curling over it, my fingers a thick wax in your heat,
the places beneath your nests of soft hair, sometimes hard
sometimes wet, the blood of your vagina so that my penis emerges
slimy and dripping red, a new birth, not entirely my own, not entirely
    me,
a red thing hanging in the air, sliding across the sheets—
we cry out at it, a thick bird dripping with blood
and more on your thighs, this flying penis the brush
and later still your finger sliding inside my crack—
as you enter me the force of your finger squeezes my orgasm out
    toward you
and my penis is personal again throbbing at my temples at my fingers in
    the tight place at my knees
and in my belly where, from the first, all the old language
was canceled out, its sounds come up new to me,
sprayed out from muscles I never knew I had, from flesh contraptions
that turned into thick whistles of air: our names
are mate and mate and something inside me kept twisting,
kept thickening itself on us, let it be, let it be dark and stony
and now under the armpits, now how your hands are a crotch
at the side of my ear, now in the way my eyelids push down hard
on your nipples, the moment when all positions disappear
and "head" and "foot" are points on a compass that's been thrown in a
    dark room by a mother full of anger.

FOR A MOMENT

I stood deep inside a willow and found it better than love.
I saw a willow's heart. It was green and easy to touch.
For a moment I was a willow-animal.
Anyone could touch me deep inside. I was easy to touch.

THE HIDDEN KNOT

Tired and depressed; once again I have hidden my sex
like a small knot in my stomach. I played with my sex
as a torturer plays with his victim.
And now the heavy arteries of blood are like stone walls.
I tear myself apart bit by bit, I suck and bite and nibble
and the small knot grows more and more hidden,
slowly it turns everything around it into a thick crust,
a wing thick with oil trapped on the beach in Santa Barbara,
at the mercy of helpful teen-agers.

I catch a sudden glimpse of myself at thirty-three walking out a door,
my hair short, carrying a briefcase and wearing the skins of a wolf as a
     cape,
triumphant, as a Roman emperor would wear the flayed skin of a
     rebellious slave leader.

THE BLOSSOMS INSIDE YOU

I climb the tree,
become a penis with fingers,
slithering and tips all over,
a horse with snakes for hooves.
White blossoms on the trees, but not like flowers,
a blooming of tight white balls,
clenching of knuckles caught in branches.
I have held a woman as she struggles to undress,
as she tries to finish what I had begun all those years ago at the
        high-school dance:
I put my arms around her as I walked down the stairs to the gym.
She shrugged me off—*not now!*
The stems beneath the blossoms snap under my fingers,
a fringe of fallen blossoms forms around the trunk.
I keep moving, picking and dropping, bunching myself smaller and
        smaller
as I crawl out on the thin newer branches.

You come.
Brown-eyed Moroccan boy, son of rich parents,
sent here to learn European culture.
I grow invisible at the top of the tree.
The white blossoms shimmer with light
as they drop slowly, one by one.
You pick them up,
stuff them into a brown leather bag,
crushing one on top of the other
with quick mechanical movements.
I say nothing, give no sign of my presence.
You are small and brown on the green grass,
down on all fours now.
The bag is full,
you cram the blossoms in your mouth like a squirrel,

then drop your trousers in one quick motion and stick them in your
    asshole.
I am almost afraid to breathe for fear you will see me,
stop spreading your cheeks with your thin brown fingers;
and shake the tree in your rage
until I too drop at your feet and you play with me and make me
    disappear.

LOST IN THE TWIN

"Well, we must hold hands tightly and hope that we can keep hold of each other through the dream and out into the waking world. . . . Could we be happy?"
She said, "This has nothing to do with happiness, nothing whatever."
—Iris Murdoch, *A Severed Head*

I am afraid of the woman in the blue-and-white dress,
that geometric pattern like a rope that zigzags round and round her
     body.
We stood in the kitchen and that dress was like a heavy veil
tossed casually across the breath of the human,
a claim on some abstract future where everything is cloth dyed into
     the shape of blue diamonds,
a world of flesh strung over wires without the flaw of blood to make
     it sing.
This was a transformation without grace,
the body still and bloated like a corpse under bright colors.

Inside the blue dress is a kitten.
I saw it in a dream drop from a tree when I clapped my hands.
Your belly swayed as you walked, always a few steps ahead of me.
I set out water for you in a tiny bowl and what I could do was done,
magician of the lost kingdom, knower of secrets not quite human.

Dream-kitten, woman-dream,
a cord connects us, placenta of dreams strangled on their own afterbirth
     and strung together.
We stumble up and down the dark stairways like zombies.
They have tied stones around our waists; under our dresses
we are shorter now and more porous.
We are only at home in the huge marble bathtub with its brass faucets
and the gold angel as plug. Here, our stones touch bottom,
we become the creek bed which sifts our flesh from us.
We rise scraped clean,
heavy with stone.

We are twins:
where one of us moves the other follows,
sullen and bewildered. One must die to free the other.
Is this why you wear the blue-and-white dress?
Was it really good-by we were saying in that kitchen?

I am terrified to lose you, to feel your body shrinking back into the
    tree.
I do not think I can follow, magic-sister,
woman I sold my suit to.
I know the tree you fell from is my own body:
you need me for a throat and I am afraid.

BROTHER   SISTER

The man in the wheelchair has long hair. He is young, a veteran, a winner who has inherited the miracle of plastic, of chrome that shines on the spokes of his wheels. He is in a room full of men, a convention of victors. A woman in a black dress moves among them. She, too, is young, American, short black hair brushed to a shine. She is working on the man in the wheelchair. Her left hand moves his penis up and down, up and down. His orgasm takes a long time. The other men do not stare, but wait their turn. Her face is strained, full of the effort of giving the cripple his orgasm.

They are in a sort of gymnasium, the basement of a Catholic church. From the street they hear the sounds of a parade, some sort of holiday. Through the windows they see the bare legs of the baton twirlers and the uniformed legs of the band players, black pants with yellow stripes and the tips of their polished black shoes.

It is almost sunset, soon the holiday will be over and the woman in black will go home to the tiny apartment she shares with her brother. Her muscles ache so much she can hardly move. Her brother rubs her shoulder and back and upper arms a long time. He hates it that she must do this, but there is no other way to survive. He is just out of prison and can't find a job. When he killed the awful man whose teeth seemed to lengthen into fangs as he laughed, the brother had no idea it would mean such suffering for his sister. But when he tells her this and apologizes she always shrugs it off and says, "You did what you had to do at the time."

IN THE NEW WORLD

for Aleksandr Solzhenitsyn

I am not sad to come back.
The inner world gives me bones—
they form themselves in silence,
they ask no questions.
They dance, they have patience.
They measure the round in years.

When I come back from the bones,
the pure fish that moves in the wind
and that has no desire;
when I come back from the pulse,
from the breath, from the belly
that delights in itself;
when I come back I am not sad.

One by one
I entered the world. The circle
of the world. My friends,
my enemies, all the streams
that needed my weight
to fall inward once again
the falls I became
poised over nothing.

This is why there is no sadness
when I come back, I come back
to this: my friends and I hold hands
in a circle. There was music,
we hurt one another,
our bones called
need, our fears
danced before our eyes,
our sex hardened,
there was no more water calling
only salt
on salt.

This is why there is no sadness.
I lick your tears,
your salt writes our names on my tongue,
our rings of salt mean forever.
Ashes cover nothing, sadness is not,
even the salt turns inward
and falls through the sunlight.
They say, *oh, the salt, the sea*,
but no, it is not that, not happiness,
not sadness.

PITT POETRY SERIES